IMAGES
of America

HELENA
MONTANA

The Queen City of the Rockies and the
Broadwater Hotel

IMAGES
of America

HELENA
MONTANA

The Queen City of the Rockies and the
Broadwater Hotel

Patricia C. Spencer

ARCADIA
PUBLISHING

Published by Arcadia Publishing
Charleston, South Carolina

Library of Congress Catalog Card Number: 2001091259

For all general information contact Arcadia Publishing at:
Telephone 843-853-2070
Fax 843-853-0044
E-mail sales@arcadiapublishing.com
For customer service and orders:
Toll-Free 1-888-313-2665

Visit us on the Internet at www.arcadiapublishing.com

This book is dedicated to my late father, Charles R. Allen, whose interest in the Broadwater inspired me to research the hotel's history and demise. Thank you, Dad, for sharing with me your interest in history, your unfaltering support, and your love.

CONTENTS

ACKNOWLEDGMENTS

For the technical assistance and editorial guidance, my sincere thanks to Keith Ulrich of Arcadia Publishing; your patience and direction were deeply appreciated. A deep appreciation and heart-felt thank you to the many people at the Montana Historical Society who helped with the various stages of this project: Lory Morrow and Becca Kohl for their assistance in selecting and identifying photos; Angela Murray for her tireless aid in verifying information and providing research assistance; and Dave Walter who has patiently guided this project from a mess of a research paper into an honors thesis and beyond. All of the photographs and images in this book come from the Montana Historical Society Photo Archive and Library Collections. Lastly, this project would not have been possible without the support of my wonderful husband who believed in my vision and encouraged me to pursue my dream, thank you.

INTRODUCTION

For decades many people have been fascinated by the fairy tale that was the Broadwater Hotel and Natatorium. The construction of the grand hotel defined the lifestyle of a generation and has continued to captivate audiences since its construction in 1889. From its conception, the grand hotel and plunge have generated questions. Why Helena? Why were so many people attracted to this tiny oasis, a mere mining camp at the time? Why was the hotel allowed to so quietly slip into our past, virtually unnoticed and unprotected?

Mystery and intrigue surrounded the deteriorating structure as the once grand hotel sat in ruins west of town on Highway 12. Long-time Helena residents would recall memories of the finer days of the hotel's existence, or share tidbits of information regarding its condition—most of which was encased in folklore or misunderstanding. Sadly, few knew or understood what had become of the fairy tale. The grand edifice is no longer a part of our physical landscape, but it is still very much a part of Helena's cultural landscape.

Little remains of the Broadwater Hotel and Natatorium except fading memories and myth. What once represented the great vision of its creator has become a field of rampant weeds and broken dreams.

Col. Charles A. Broadwater, a man of vision and hope, demonstrated an extraordinary faith in Helena. The *Helena Independent* described Broadwater as "very near to the best life of Helena, and his manner of expressing his faith in the city was as big and fluent as his name." The Colonel dreamed of constructing a magnificent hotel to reflect Helena's elegance and his commitment to the city's future.

Sadly, Broadwater's elaborate objective never would be fulfilled. Events and circumstances worked against the hotel's success from the moment of its conception. Historian Bob Fletcher reflected in *Montana: The Magazine of Western History* in 1953, 30 years after the hotel's demise, that despite the Colonel's faith in Helena and his dream, the "hotel was never a financial success and opened and closed several times." No single event or person can be blamed for the failure of the grand resort. Rather, a series of events combined to create the hotel's failure.

The Broadwater Hotel symbolized elegance second to none in the world. Yet much more underlies the hotel than a mere dream, notably the man himself. The events of Broadwater's life reflect the traditional rags-to-riches story. Hard work, perseverance, and a keen business sense resulted in success throughout his life.

Col. Charles A. Broadwater was a self-made man involved in nearly every aspect of pioneer Montana. From 1862 to 1886, Broadwater built a financial empire through various business ventures ranging from cattle to wagon freighting, to banking, politics, and finally railroads. Broadwater's alliance with James J. Hill and the Great Northern Railroad dramatically altered his political and business relationships. It was Colonel Broadwater's involvement in the emerging rail lines in the 1884 Montana Territory that led to the construction of the hotel and natatorium.

Colonel Broadwater devoted a great deal of energy and time to the development of railroads in Montana. Contemporary historians cite Broadwater's railroad involvement as the driving force in the creation of the hotel. Broadwater initially purchased the land to thwart rivals laying tracks in the area. The effort failed, however, and he looked for a lucrative alternative for the property. A clever businessman, the Colonel realized the potential of the location and utilized his land to create a first-class resort.

The era in which the Broadwater Hotel and Hot Springs flourished became as critical to its existence as the man himself. A closer study of the "Gay Nineties," or Gilded Age, will reveal the people, styles, and attitudes that shaped the elaborate hotel, as well as the changing times, attitudes, and values that reshaped its function and purpose. As events unfolded, the hotel could neither withstand nor adapt to widespread and drastic change.

After Broadwater's death, the hotel endured a series of alterations and changes of ownership. Inconsistencies in management and ownership created the ultimate tragedy leading to the final closure of the hotel in the 1940s. A natural disaster, the changing economic and social climate of Helena, and advancements in travel combined to render the once elegant hotel obsolete. Unfortunately, the fairy tale that constituted the story of the Broadwater lacks the traditional happy ending.

One

CHARLES A. BROADWATER:
ENTREPRENEUR AND HELENA VISIONARY

Col. Charles A. Broadwater epitomized the self-made man. Born on September 25, 1840, to Charles Henry and Anne Broadwater, young Charles grew up on his father's cotton plantation just outside of St. Charles, Missouri. As a youth Charles worked in a St. Louis mercantile house, where he learned basic business and accounting practices. In 1861, at the age of 21, Charles grew tired of his limiting surroundings and looking to avoid involvement in the Civil War, he acted on his desire to venture west.

The 1860s represented a time of exploration and discovery in the Trans-Mississippi West. Rich mines and endless land provided boundless opportunities that created millionaires overnight. Young Charles arrived on this scene in 1862. Gold recently had been discovered in Bannack, located in the eastern district of Idaho territory (the area would become the western Montana Territory in 1864). An area rich in mineral potential, it attracted men from all over the West. Broadwater recognized the area's economic possibilities and seized the opportunity to capitalize on that potential. Thus Charles A. Broadwater, the entrepreneur, emerged.

Broadwater was a member of Montana's pioneer generation, and his career reflected the American success story—the ascent to riches. From 1862 to 1886, Broadwater built a business empire through numerous ventures.

He began his expansive Montana career, which would span 30 years, by selling cattle to, and trading horses with, local miners. In 1862 he formed a partnership with capitalist John J. Pemberton and platted the settlement of Cottonwood (present-day Deer Lodge), Montana.

In 1863 Broadwater gained employment with a fledgling operation known as the Diamond R Freighting Company. Soon the superintendent of the Diamond R, Broadwater became a leading figure in Montana's growing transportation industry. The last series of Colonel Broadwater's business ventures linked him closely to the bustling frontier town of Helena, in Montana Territory. Broadwater embraced Helena as his home, both professionally and personally. In 1866 he relocated the headquarters of the Diamond R to the city. Historian Nedra Bayne described Broadwater's affection for Helena as one of guiding dedication toward the people of his state, and particularly those of his chosen city.

The Colonel led an expansive life. He reached Montana in her pioneer days and accompanied the state to prosperity. As a businessman and resident, he never lost sight of the area's potential.

Broadwater and partner John J. Pemberton engaged in a horse-trading business. The two men remained partners, active in various business ventures in the Cottonwood (Deer Lodge) and Bannack areas, until 1863. In that year Broadwater purchased cattle in the Cottonwood area and sold them at a considerable profit in Bannack. Despite this lucrative venture, Broadwater pursued other opportunities in the growing transportation business.

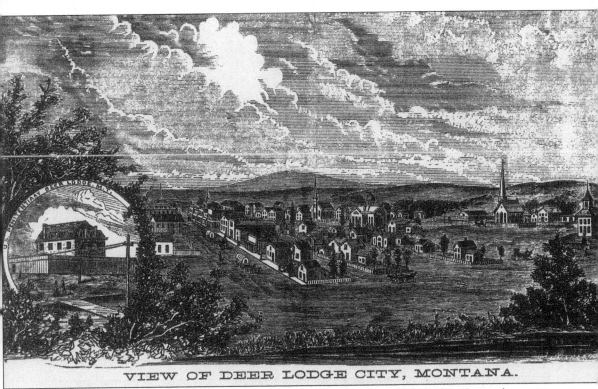

VIEW OF DEER LODGE CITY, MONTANA.

Cattlemen preceded miners to the Montana Territory before the 1860s Gold Rush. Southwestern Montana provided the optimal location for raising beef, and cattlemen soon began a lucrative trade with migrants on the Oregon Trail. By the time migrants reached the Wyoming and Montana Territories their cattle was road-weary and hungry. Cattlemen would trade one of their healthy cows for two of the Oregon Trail stock, creating a lucrative commerce for local ranchers. Cattle ranches grew in size and wealth, and as a result Deer Lodge grew into a cattle community nestled in the Deer Lodge Valley, as this 1879 picture depicts.

11

First Territorial governor Sidney Edgerton chose Bannack as the temporary capital in 1864 and ordered the first territorial legislature to meet there.

By 1865 the capital had been moved to Virginia City, the center of the territory's population. As Virginia City's population began to decline and residents began to search out prominence and prestige for their towns, the capital question once again arose. A struggle between Helena and Virginia City ensued over location of the capital. An 1867 election resulted in Virginia City's remaining capital, but by 1874 Helena was clearly the center of activity in the territory. Pictured is Wallace Street, Virginia City, in the Montana Territory of the early 1870s.

After a hotly contested election and a ruling by the Montana Supreme Court, Helena was named the capital of the Montana Territory in 1875. The new capital city, centrally located, containing rich quartz mines, and located on a projected rail route, was poised to grow into a metropolitan city.

In 1869 Broadwater merged with Matt Carroll, George Steell, and E.G. Maclay to purchase the Diamond R. Under Broadwater's direction, the Diamond R dominated Montana carrying trade. At its height, the freighting company owned 300 wagons, 350 mules, and 500 yoke of oxen. The Diamond R remained under Broadwater's leadership until the 1880s, when railroads rendered wagon freighting considerably less profitable on major routes.

Created in 1864, the Diamond R Freighting Company quickly came to dominate local carrying trade. The company provided service throughout the Territory. Despite the high overhead costs, the Diamond R turned a large profit, making a fortune for its owners. Here, Diamond R wagons deliver goods to Miles City in 1880.

The U.S. Army contracted the Diamond R to haul materials to Fort Assinniboine (near present-day Havre) and to Fort Maginnis (northeast of Lewistown), under construction in 1873. Upon their completion, Broadwater maintained trading posts at both locations. He built this home at Fort Assinniboine. While doing this contract work for the Army, Broadwater acquired the title of "Colonel," although he never actually served in the military.

The Army built Fort Assinniboine on the northwestern slopes of the Bearpaw Mountains, due to tensions in the area between White settlers, the Metis Indians, and the presence of Sitting Bull. The $1 million fort grew to become one of the West's major military bases. The fort's impressive brick architecture quickly became the center of regional operations for the Army and the headquarters for the District of Montana. By 1880, Broadwater's trader's store was a vital part of the fort's operations.

The 1880s in Montana witnessed dramatic political alliances that radically changed and shaped territorial politics and eventually statehood. Four influential Montana businessmen and politicians led the Territory's Democratic party in the 1880s: Samuel T. Hauser, "Copper Kings" William A. Clark and Marcus Daly, and Col. Charles A. Broadwater. Montana's Democratic "Big Four" wielded an influence as strong as the machine bosses in more eastern regions.

Helena rapidly became the banking center of Montana in the early 1870s, and remained so until the Panic of 1893. Among other contributions to the city, Broadwater opened the Montana National Bank in November 1882. Leading Montana capitalist A.H. Wilder, governor Benjamin Potts, and senator Russell Harrison capitalized on the "Golden Age of Banking" and provided the $250,000 capital for the bank.

The posh interior of the Montana National Bank reflected the wealth of the growing city.

Friend and business associate James J. Hill once teased Broadwater that he was investing too much money in Helena and that buffalo would wander down Main Street before the city gained financial success. As a monument to his faith in Helena, and to refute Hill, Broadwater placed a keystone buffalo-head above the entrance of his bank. In 1888 the Montana National Bank displayed the "largest gold bar in the world." The bar weighed 6,945 ounces, worth $100,000.

A powerful factor in the financial affairs of the state, the Montana National Bank directly challenged other financial institutions in Helena, particularly Samuel T. Hauser's First National Bank. Hauser viewed the Montana National as a threat to his lucrative Northern Pacific Railroad Company account. The establishment of the Montana National signified the beginning of many conflicts between Hauser and Broadwater. On July 27, 1893, both Hauser's First National and Broadwater's Montana National closed due to the Panic of 1893. The Montana National Bank later merged with First National to become First National Bank and Trust Company and later First Bank.

Samuel T. Hauser, known as a shrewd banker and the most important Democrat in the territory, served briefly as governor during the 1880s. He apparently resigned after a dispute with the U.S. land commissioner.

Fire destroyed the original Montana National Bank building in 1944. Two women died and eight others were injured in the blaze.

The First National Bank and Trust Company built a new building on the corner of Sixth and Main in the 1930s, replacing a farm implement firm built in 1883 by S.C. Ashby and Colonel Broadwater. The Montana Club and the Federal Building (now the City-County Building) highlight the area.

Designed by architect J.M. Paulsen, the original Montana Club Building was esteemed as Montana's finest showpiece. Organized in 1885 for "gentlemen only," and only those gentlemen who were millionaires, the Montana Club held its grand opening in April 1895 with 130 members. By 1888 membership had grown to 160 members and the expanding club moved from its quarters in the Parchen Block to the Gold Block. With membership rising, the club decided to build its own facility and purchased a lot on the corner of Sixth and Fuller. Built in 1893, the seven-story social club functioned to advertise Helena as a "prosperous and progressive city." The fashionable club contained a reading room, a dining room, a bowling alley, and many of the club's members kept offices in the building.

Fire destroyed the Montana Club early on the morning of April 28, 1903. It was soon discovered that 14-year old Harry Anderson had intentionally set the fire. Fascinated by fire, Anderson routinely hung around local fires watching the firemen do their work. When questioned about the fire, Anderson admitted that he had "an uncontrollable desire to see the horses run and to help the firemen work." Anderson was sentenced to the state reform school at Miles City until the age of 21. Ironically, Anderson's father Julian worked as the club's bartender from 1893–1953, and became a prominent part of the club's history.

Club members rallied to replace the destroyed building and immediately hired architect Cass Gilbert to design a new building. The "new" Montana Club opened in the summer of 1905 with a formal dedication held on December 30, 1905. The seven-story building featured a library, billiard room, meeting rooms, a card room, private apartments for bachelor members, and dining facilities. Despite economic hardships, the club has managed to stay in continuous operation.

Colonel Broadwater also invested in the development of Last Chance Gulch from a mining camp into a thriving city. In addition to the Montana National Bank, Broadwater owned the Broadwater Business Block on the corner of Main and Sixth. The business block featured the Goodkind Brothers wholesale liquors and J. Blockwood, wholesale and retail druggist. The middle portion of the block was lost to fire in 1928 but the Goodkind building remains intact.

Photographer F.J. Haynes photographed Helena in 1894 for the Northern Pacific Railway and provided the following description of the bustling city: "Helena has a population of about 13,000, is the capital of Montana, and the county seat of Lewis and Clark county. It is the natural distributing and business center of the state. The city has some fine public buildings including the Capitol, Federal Buildings, Court House, Public Library, Churches, Schools, and Hospitals. It is a city of Homes, many of the businessmen, stockmen, woolgrowers, and miners whose varied interests are in other parts of the state, making their homes here. There is a considerable manufacturing and it is the center of one of the richest gold producing districts in the west. The Broadwater Natatorium, a pleasure and health resort, is located in the suburbs of the city. Being situated in the foothills of the main range of the Rockies, it is shielded from severe storms and the climate is delightful and invigorating the year around. Last Chance Gulch in which Helena is built is an old placer field that has produced $50,000,000 or more in clean gold."

Helena, the "Queen City of the Rockies," boasted the most millionaire's per-capita in the 1890s. Accordingly, businessmen and ranchers built fine homes in the city's upper west side as testimony to the area's wealth and potential. Broadwater purchased this home as a gift for his wife, Julia, in 1884, although the Broadwater's had been living there since 1878. Fire consumed the rear wing of the home in 1898. Mrs. Broadwater sold the residence in 1910. Built about 1872, the mansion—on the corner of North Benton and Holter avenues—burnt to the ground on January 12, 1917.

Colonel Broadwater married Julia C. Chumasero, daughter of Judge William Chumasero, in 1873. The couple had two children, Charles C. and Wilder.

30

Two

RAILROADS, LUXURY RESORTS, AND HELENA

Cargo transporting proved to be a lucrative business venture for many Montana businessmen. Col. Charles A. Broadwater capitalized on these possibilities early, first in wagon freighting and later in railroading. His railroad connections began through mining ventures in the Helena area, while his expectations later expanded to include tourism prospects and the development of his famous hot springs.

Colonel Broadwater's railroad involvement began in the mid-1870s. Federal land-grant money allocated to the Northern Pacific Railroad allowed the line to forge west. Broadwater recognized early the importance of the Helena valley to the westward expansion of rail lines.

Wishing to develop Montana resources, Broadwater entered into a partnership and business alliance with railroad mogul James J. Hill. Hill, the president of the St. Paul, Minneapolis, and Manitoba Railway (later the Great Northern Railway), sought to extend his northern-plains line west from Devil's Lake, Dakota Territory. His ultimate goal was to reach the West Coast. Broadwater, familiar with Montana politics, business, and freighting transportation, became Hill's "point man" in the territory. He kept Hill apprised of financial and political developments, and in essence, served as the inside man and public relations agent for the Manitoba in Montana.

Broadwater's involvement with Hill and the Manitoba dissolved local political alliances for the Colonel. Entrepreneur Samuel T. Hauser and Broadwater had long been friends and political allies, and both were members of the Democratic "Big Four." By 1888, however, Broadwater and Hauser's relationship had disintegrated. The Northern Pacific had completed its main line through to the Pacific Coast by 1883, and Hauser held strong business ties to the NP. As president of the First National Bank in Helena, Hauser secured the lucrative Northern Pacific account. Hauser feared that Broadwater's Montana National Bank would steal this valued client.

Not a recipient of federal land-grant funds like the NP, the Manitoba depended upon settlement and immediate freighting to recoup its construction investments. In an effort to attract Hill to Montana, Broadwater promoted the rich silver deposits in the Red Mountain mining district, west of Helena (near Rimini). This could provide the raw material caches that Hill sought for his line's development. Hill also intended his rail line to tap the copper ore of Butte. Montana Territory promised lucrative ventures for J.J. Hill.

31

In 1884 Hill and his investors established the Montana Central Railway to connect Butte, Helena, and Great Falls by rail. The Montana Central, a corporation separate from the Manitoba, was recognized as a complementary line and it operated under Hill's complete control.

Northern Pacific officials, already monopolizing Montana commerce, resented the Manitoba's incursion into what they perceived as "their territory." As a result, between 1884 and 1886, a heated feud developed between the two railroad giants. The battles included disputes over the control of lucrative mining claims, local finances, and pivotal right-of-way properties.

Broadwater's 1874 acquisition of land at the mouth of Ten Mile Canyon, just west of Helena, proved vital for the Manitoba in its attempt to block the Northern Pacific's progress. Due to the natural formation of the area, only a limited rail-line grade was possible. Therefore, since Broadwater and the Manitoba held control of the canyon, the NP's progress appeared to be blocked.

Conflict between the two rail companies led to disputes and court injunctions throughout 1886. Broadwater appealed to the Montana Supreme Court over the Montana Central's right-of-way privileges. The court ruled in favor of Broadwater, forcing the NP to find another grade to complete its line through to Rimini.

Victory over the NP in the Red Mountain mining district placed Hill, the Montana Central, and the Manitoba in a position of dominance in Montana Territory railroad expansion. The Montana Central completed its line from Butte to Helena in the autumn of 1886, and from Helena to Great Falls in 1887. By the fall of 1887, Broadwater's line had connected with the western end of the Manitoba line, and the cross-country line spread from the Dakota Territory to Montana.

The Manitoba needed to recuperate financially from its massive capital outlay, and a truce with the NP would aid in that recuperation. Beginning in 1886, a softening in the conflict between the two companies occurred. A decrease in tensions led to concessions by both rail lines.

With the truce, Broadwater sought alternative uses for his land. A saloon and bathhouse operated on the property, and the Colonel extrapolated the bathhouse concept to include an extravagant resort complete with a health spa.

Charles Broadwater, an astute businessman, capitalized on the opportunities proved by the emerging rail business. Never to allow a venture to languish, he redirected his intent after he lost the Rimini line to the NP. The magnificent Broadwater Hotel and Natatorium, a product of the Colonel's ingenuity, resulted from the unsuccessful Manitoba-Montana Central attempt to profit from the Red Mountain mining district.

Remains of downtown Helena after the August 1872 fire. Fire broke out at the Northern Pacific hotel and destroyed six commercial blocks.

Access to the Red Mountain mining district played a key role in the ensuing battle between the Northern Pacific and the Manitoba. Whichever company gained control of the district stood to acquire great financial opportunities. The two lines competed for mining claims and raced to complete a branch line from Helena to Rimini. From 1874 through 1886 Broadwater acquired the titles to property at strategic points along the Helena-Rimini right-of-way. Due to the high cost of completing the Montana Central line, Hill surrendered the right-of-way to the Rimini-Red Mountain mining district to the NP. The railway immediately established the Helena and Red Mountain Railroad Company, with Samuel T. Hauser as president. The line began operation of the 16-mile track in December 1886.

In 1874 Broadwater purchased 80 acres west of Helena on Ten Mile Creek. The property proved to be a pivotal area, for it straddled Ten Mile Canyon and could block movement through the defile. Ferdinand and Caroline Wassweiler, needing money to cover Ferdinand's heavy gambling debt, sold the land, rights to the hot springs, and the Hot Springs Hotel to Broadwater for $10,500. The Colonel maintained the hotel and saloon until 1889, when his new hotel and health spa opened.

The old Hot Springs Hotel on Ten Mile Creek operated from 1869 to 1889. The original, smaller hotel catered to local miners and served as a place where they could rest and recuperate after a six-day workweek. Recuperation consisted of a substantial hot meal, a rejuvenating bath, and whatever other "pleasures" the hotel staff offered.

The proliferation of railroads and growing tourism in the West during the 1880s generated a renewed interest in the profitability of thermal and hot springs. With the Great Northern Depot centrally located in downtown Helena (pictured here in the 1920s), and the Northern Pacific Depot prominently located on the eastside (opposite page, 1885), Broadwater believed that transcontinental railroads would bring unlimited tourists to his grand resort.

Colonel Broadwater's strong faith in the impact of railroads led to the creation of the Broadwater Hotel and Natatorium. His miscalculation of the railroads' ability to create and sustain "destination resorts" is the single most noted cause for the failure of the hotel. However,, this misconception represented only one of several fatal problems for the Colonel's dream.

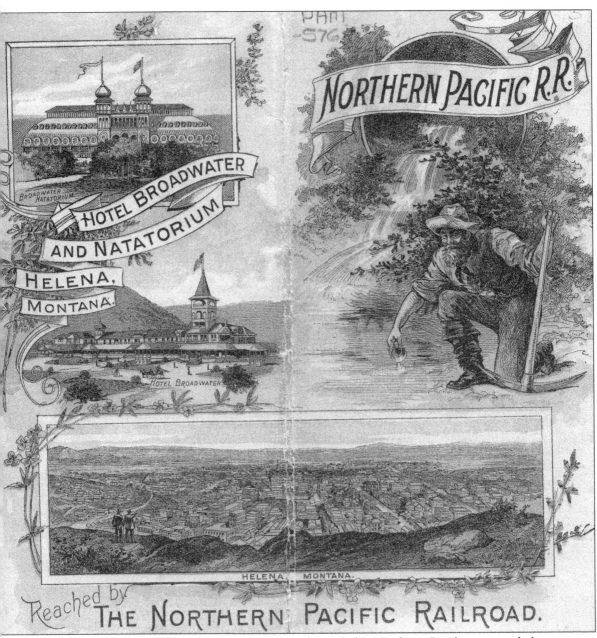

NORTHERN Pacific R.R.

HOTEL BROADWATER AND NATATORIUM HELENA, MONTANA.

BROADWATER NATATORIUM.

HOTEL BROADWATER

HELENA, MONTANA.

Reached by THE NORTHERN PACIFIC RAILROAD.

The reciprocal concession between the Manitoba and the Northern Pacific prompted the publication of the Northern Pacific's "Hotel Broadwater and Natatorium" brochure in 1891. The brochure advertised the luxurious hotel and its many offerings. Most importantly, the brochure contained information necessary to plan a trip by rail, via the Northern Pacific, to Helena and the Hotel Broadwater.

HOTEL BROADWATER

Health for You and Pleasure Too

NATURAL HOT SPRINGS
of HEALTH-GIVING WATERS
SITUATED IN THE HEART of
THE ROCKY MOUNTAINS

*THE TRUE CARLSBAD
OF AMERICA*

BROADWATER NATATORIUM

Helena Hot Springs Company
HELENA, MONTANA

The Helena Hot Springs Company tried to attract tourists from the east by marketing the resort as "The True Carlsbad of America."

Broadwater's railroad ventures also led to a local, lucrative steam and electric trolley line. The Helena Electric Railway Company transported passengers from downtown Helena out to the Kessler Brewery, Central Park, and the Broadwater Hotel and Natatorium. This c. 1889 trolley bears the destination "Helena Hot Springs and Smelter." The c. 1890 trolley below advertises the "Hotel Broadwater and the Great Swimming Bath."

The Helena Street Railway began providing Helenans with reliable service on September 25, 1886. Electric trolleys replaced the horse drawn Pullman cars in 1888. In 1927 the Helena Electric Railway Company reorganized as the Helena Gas and Electric Company in 1927. Trolley service ended at midnight on January 1, 1928, when bus service replaced the perceived outdated mode of trolley transportation.

Colonel Broadwater's trolley delivers guests to the luxurious natatorium. Broadwater's son, C.C., is pictured on the front of the trolley.

Broadwater was devoted to the development of Helena, but his belief in the area would not be enough to sustain the challenges faced by the young city. Between 1872 and 1894, the city rose from the remains of its third fire into a bustling economic and transportation center.

As Helenans anxiously waited for the dawning of the new century, crisis again gripped their city. More fires, financial devastation, and the relocation of the economic center to Butte would challenge the growth and prosperity of the former mining camp.

By 1894 Last Chance Gulch had transformed from a muddy mining camp into a metropolitan city, complete with an electric trolley line. Most of the buildings along the Gulch bore the name of Helena's influential businessmen, such as the Power block (right corner) and the Broadwater block (left).

Three

THE CONSTRUCTION
OF A DREAM

*I*n the late summer of 1888, Charles A. Broadwater commenced the greatest project of his career, the construction of a hotel and hot springs resort unlike any other in the world. The dream became the most costly of the Colonel's business ventures and the least successful.

Colonel Broadwater poured large amounts of money into the project to guarantee that his extraordinary resort would rival all others in elegance. The Helena Independent reported on September 9, 1888, that "this hotel is to be just what Helena needs—a respectable, healthful, and luxurious place of resort." Original estimates figured the cost of completion for both structures at $100,000. Construction began in August 1888, with completion scheduled for the following spring.

Changes in plans and delays increased the cost of construction. The final expenditures totaled $500,000. Broadwater invested $50,000 alone to pipe the needed combination of mineral and cool spring waters into the natatorium. Other expenses included: the hotel, with furnishings, $259,795; the finished natatorium and plunge, $97,000; landscaping, $20,000; machinery, ground preparation, and roads, $100,000.

Finally on August 26, 1889, one year after construction began, the hotel opened its doors to the Helena community. The Helena Daily Herald exclaimed on August 27, 1889, that Broadwater had provided them with "a hotel [they could] be proud of." Colonel Broadwater planned no formal grand-opening ceremonies to inaugurate the new hotel. The Democratic convention in Anaconda and the Territory's impending statehood diverted his attention from Helena. So the citizens of Helena, proud of the new resort and thankful of Broadwater, arranged for the opening gala themselves. The Board of Trade and the City Council planned an impromptu excursion and opening ceremony to honor Broadwater and his latest contribution to Helena.

The Helena City Council christened the new structure the Hotel Broadwater and gave a hearty thanks to the Colonel, who had transformed the area from an arid waste and tangled wilderness into a paradise. The citizens of Helena believed that the Hotel Broadwater and the Natatorium stood as a monument to Charles Broadwater that would never fade.

Despite, or perhaps because of, all the charm, elegance, modern facilities, and medicinal qualities of the Broadwater, the hotel never operated at a profit. The high cost of equipment and construction, in addition to Montana's small population at the time, caused Broadwater to operate the hotel for a number of years without profit and at a great expense.

Broadwater's death in 1892 signaled the beginning of many problems that plagued the young resort during that decade. Ownership of the property transferred seven different times between 1892 and 1945, and the resort complex suffered a variety of face-lifts.

The 1890s brought irregular but measured growth and prosperity to Montana and the rest of the nation. The Gay Nineties flourished with lavishness and elegance. As historian Frederick Jackson Turner's highly proclaimed frontier closed, America advanced beyond even its own expectations. Progress dominated the era. Technological advancements, hints of social reform, and concerted economic expansion highlighted the dawn of the 20th century.

Within this context Broadwater built his dream, a context in which the dream might well have thrived. Yet economic frustrations overshadowed the achievements of the early 1890s. Montana, the second largest producer of silver, fell from economic prominence with the repeal of the Sherman Silver Purchase Act in 1893. Sadly, the hotel would not withstand the decade, nor could it maintain the elegant facade of an era rapidly receding into the American past.

An early advertisement for the hotel Broadwater, boasting the resort's "Aquatic Theatre" and "Mineral Springs."

The Natatorium
at
Hot Springs,
near Helena, MS.

Broadwater commissioned two separate architectural companies to design and to construct the two components of his resort. The architectural firm of Wallace, Thornburgh, and Appleton drafted plans for the proposed hotel, with Herman Kemna overseeing the construction. Design and direction for the Moorish Natatorium originated within the architectural firm of John C. Paulson and Noah J. McConnell. Different architects ensured distinct designs of elegance and, indeed, the two structures held no resemblance to one another.

Approximately 500 people attended the opening ceremony on the evening of August 26, 1889. Broadwater's steam streetcar line provided transportation for 400 celebrants from downtown Helena to the hotel. Visitors paid $1.25 per person for transportation, dinner, and entertainment. Thirty-five guests even booked overnight reservations in the hotel.

In its original splendor, the Broadwater Hotel and Natatorium achieved its goal as a first class resort. Caretakers carefully landscaped the property with rare and exotic plants. Grounds

adorned with fountains, benches, swings, and a cottonwood grove handsomely complemented
the hotel and natatorium. An abundance of outdoor activities provided recreation for the

guests, including horseback rides, hikes up nearby Mt. Helena, paddleboat trips around the lake, croquet, tennis, and simple relaxation on the veranda encircling the hotel. The hotel contained

50 guest rooms, 40 private bath chambers, a billiard parlor, a ballroom, 3 dining rooms, a bar, and 2 sitting parlors.

Two weeks after the August 26th opening, the new hotel and natatorium closed for the season to complete the adjacent grounds and natatorium. Landscapers added a man-made lake to the property before it opened for its second season. Lake Thermal, also referred to as Wilder Lake, measured a 1/3 mile long and 12 feet deep. Located northwest of the natatorium, fresh mountain-spring water piped from Ten Mile Creek filled the lake and was intended to provide guests with the opportunity to take a leisurely canoe or paddleboat ride.

Helena Hot Springs and Mt. Helena, Helena, Mont.

The modest exterior of the hotel hid an elegant and extravagant interior. The 1891 Northern Pacific Railroad brochure trumpeted the wonders of the Hotel Broadwater and Natatorium: "In entering the hotel, the ascending staircase, the office, the halls with cozy corners, the reception-rooms, the parlors and all, combine to produce that restful and home-like effect so cheery to the weary traveler or invalid."

Broadwater decorated and furnished the hotel's interior with the finest items money could buy. Cherry, walnut, oak, and mahogany furnished each room of the hotel. Upholstery varied from horsehair and satin to tapestry. Wilton velvets, Turkish rugs, and tapestries decorated floors and walls. Inviting easy chairs and soft couches called guests to relax and enjoy their rich surroundings. Radiators in each room insured that a comfortable temperature would be maintained year round. Lavish fixtures adorned each suite and room. Elegant washstands of marble with brass plumbing fixtures supplied each guest room with spring and cool water. An Italian-marble tub with one-quarter-inch gold inlay rivaled the other elegant fixtures as the showpiece of Colonel Broadwater's suite, later the bridal suite.

Elegantly furnished and beautifully presented, the Broadwater's main dining room offered fare comparable to any esteemed European hotel. Each evening guest enjoyed an 8-to-10 course meals served on fine china and Reed and Barton silver and cutlery engraved with the establishment's name. Waiters in full-dress suites seated and served guests at tables draped with Damask tablecloths. A la carte fares proved options for guests with special dietary concerns. A diner could gaze over the magnificent grounds through bay windows of beveled glass with cut-crystal decorations. Adjacent to the main dining hall, two smaller dining rooms accommodated extra guests and private parties. Together the two areas served 115 guests. In each dining facility the furniture could easily be removed and a dance floor created. The hotel also contained a billiard parlor, a barbershop, a ballroom, a bar, and two sitting parlors. The Broadwater contained almost everything that a guest could want or need.

During its golden age, the hotel employed maids, butlers, chefs, and cleaning personnel. As seasonal employees, the staff often left the area in search of employment and was replaced by new workers in the spring.

Intricate windows of stained glass decorated both the hotel and the natatorium; the hotel alone contained 160 such windows. Electric lights brightened the entire complex, allowing visitors all the comforts of the most modern advancements. At night, when the electric lights glowed through the natatorium's stained-glass windows and dome, they illuminated a "scene of Oriental magnificence such as we dreamed of when reading Arabian Nights."

If the intricate woodwork and design of the cottage-like hotel overwhelmed visitors, it paled in comparison to the Moorish architecture of the natatorium. Billed as the "largest and most elegant piscine or plunge bath in the world," the natatorium provided both relaxation and recuperation. The pool measured 300 feet by 125 feet wide and a well-kept walk ran parallel to the pool on either side. An observation deck above the dressing rooms allowed guests to gaze down upon swimmers and the spray fountain in the center of the pool.

Mountain spring water, as well as water from the hot springs, cascaded over granite boulders piled 40 feet high into the pool below.

Designed as a health spa for the elite, the natatorium claimed to improve health. Advertisements proclaimed that the thermal waters of the Broadwater surpassed other hot springs in the U.S., for they were also medicinal.

For those guests who desired a secluded bath, the hotel housed 40 private bath chambers, evenly divided for male and female patrons. Each chamber contained an imported French silver-trimmed porcelain tub on marble feet. The private chambers furnished a comfortable lounge for relaxation after the bath. Privacy allowed the visitor to enjoy a bath of even temperature for as long as they desired.

The internationally renowned needle bath, or "Universal douche," became another attraction of the Broadwater. Patrons could be sprayed from all directions with water jets of any temperature desired.

The cottage-style hotel is pictured from atop of the natatorium. Electric lamps provided paths with gentle light, allowing guests to take romantic strolls after dinner on summer evenings.

Montanan's embarked on the 19th century's "Gay Nineties" with their state emerging as the "young giant of the Northwest." Helena had established a wealth and elegance comparable to any bustling cosmopolitan area of the time. The city of 13,834 citizens boasted the "wealthiest per capita population in the world," reported the *Helena Weekly Herald* on August 29, 1889. Helena's new mansions exemplified all of the comforts and sophistication of the East with a Western charm. Men and women regaling in the fine clothing of the times often enjoyed a sunny afternoon on the grounds of the hotel and natatorium, a tribute to the era.

Mrs. Broadwater (second from left) and her daughter, Wilder (front), often entertained the city's elite at the natatorium.

Wilder Broadwater and a friend on the grounds of the hotel. Once the hotel was completed, Broadwater lived in his private suite most of the year. Other notable Helena families, such as the Power's, the Hauser's, the Holter's, and the Ashby's, resided in fancy suites at the Broadwater during the summer months.

"The Boy with the Leaky Boot" fountain proudly welcomed guests into the natatorium. One of only seven fountains like it in the world, it remains on display at the old First National Bank in downtown Helena.

PIONEERS

— OF —

MONTANA.

1864.   1889.

ADMIT BEARER TO BANQUET

— AT —

Hotel Broadwater

Saturday Evening, Aug. 31, 1889.

W. F. SANDERS.   S. T. HAUSER.   CORNELIUS HEDGES.
          A. M. HOLTER.   S. H. CROUNSE

After Broadwater's death, his resort complex remained a destination for state political leaders. On August 31, 1899, the Pioneers of Montana hosted a lavish, by invitation only, banquet at the hotel.

The Broadwater Hotel and Natatorium stood as a symbol of Helena's magnificence and a fine complement to the high spirits of the era in Montana. The grand resort existed "when folks took the time to appreciate the beautiful and enjoy their own lives," explained historian John Ellingsen.

During this period the Broadwater might well have flourished. However, beginning in 1892 the hotel endured a series of tragedies that seriously rocked its solid foundation.

Charles A. Broadwater died on May 25, 1892, only 30 years after his arrival in Montana, and less than three years after his dream became a reality. The May 25, 1892, *Helena Daily Herald* credited Colonel Broadwater with, "making this city what it now is, and in opening the way for its limitless future." Broadwater contributed much to his beloved Helena, yet his passing drew mourners more because of his personality than his business accomplishments. His obituary proclaimed, "He was one of nature's noblemen—a kindly, genial, courteous gentleman. His memory will be fondly and gratefully cherished by the people of Helena."

More than 5,000 people attended Broadwater's funeral on May 29, 1892, the largest funeral held in the state up to that time. Area businesses closed for the day and flags were lowered to half-mast as a symbol of respect for the Colonel. Helena Masonic Lodge No. 3, A.F. and A.M., in which Broadwater had been active for many years, arranged for and provided the funeral services. The funeral of full Masonic ritual concluded at Forestvale Cemetery. Broadwater's death impacted the entire state. Four special trains carried mourners to Helena from all over the state and country specifically for the Colonel's funeral.

Broadwater's beautiful resort west of town produced the greatest pleasure for the Colonel at the end of his life. From the grand veranda encircling the hotel, Broadwater watched local families enjoying a Sunday outing. Although the Colonel had created a first-class hotel, it pleased him

that all people could enjoy the beautiful resort. The natatorium was a popular spot for local residents on weekends. Patrons could rent bathing suits and spend the day frolicking in the soothing spring water.

The Colonel's elegant resort had been designed to attract tourists from afar. Only accessible via the horse-and-buggy and rail lines, the hotel quickly became dependent upon local tourists

to turn a profit. Changing modes of transportation, an economic downturn, and harsh winters made this reliance on local tourism risky.

Pictured are ladies and gentlemen of the "Gay Nineties" enjoying an afternoon at the Broadwater Hotel and Natatorium, 1898.

Four

HELENA'S EMERGENCE AS THE CAPITAL CITY

By 1890 commercial buildings and electric lights lined the streets of downtown Helena. Electric streetcars carried residents up and down a Main Street that only a short time before had been a muddy mining camp. The progress highlighted the Queen City's recent growth from a remote frontier into a metropolitan location.

As Helena quickly became the population and economic center of the state, a bitter dispute over placement of the territorial capital arose. Bannack served as the territory's first capital after territorial governor Sidney Edgerton had ordered the legislature to convene there in 1864. The next year, legislators moved the capital to the bustling mining camp of Virginia City. Immediately a bitter struggle ensued between supporters of Virginia City and supporters of Helena for capital. An election to determine the seat of government's location was held in 1869. Speculation of fraud and a mysterious fire destroyed the ballots. A third election in 1874 also failed to resolve the dispute. Amid accusations of fraud, ballots from Gallatin and Meagher counties were thrown out resulting in a legal battle. After the U.S. Supreme Court refused to hear the case on appeal, the Montana Supreme Court resolved the situation by naming Helena the capital city of Montana Territory in 1875.

Location of the state capital once again became an issue after Montana gained statehood in 1889. The state's new constitution left the determination of a permanent capital up to the vote of the people. No single city received enough votes in the 1892 election to resolve the issue, resulting in a special runoff election in November of 1894. The election focused on Helena and the mining town of Anaconda as contenders for the seat of government.

Again, the contest became embittered in scandal. Copper Kings and political rivals William A. Clark and Marcus Daly became embroiled in a battle over the placement of the permanent capital. Daly desired his company town of Anaconda to become the center of Montana politics and spent an estimated $2.5 million dollars on the campaign. Clark, believing that the temporary capital should become the permanent one, placed his financial support behind Helena's bid for capital city. Daly and his supporters shunned Helena as a viable choice due to its high society and cultural pretensions, while Clark's supporter's targeted Daly's control of Anaconda and its people as reason not to be selected for the capital.

Residents of Helena and Anaconda held gala parades to promote their city, while Clark and Daly showered residents with free liquor and cash. Despite the extravagant campaigning, Daly and Anaconda lost the battle by nearly 2,000 votes. Clark's victory train received a hero's welcome as it arrived in Helena. A parade of nearly 15,000 wound its way down the former mining camp in celebration while a bonfire atop Mount Helena lit the city streets. Helena saloons served everyone free drinks and toasted an elated Clark for his efforts in securing the Queen City as the Treasure State's capital city.

After 25 years of being a Territory, Montana became the 41st state in 1889. In November of 1894 Montanan's selected Helena as the permanent capital and preparations began for the construction of a statehouse. Ground breaking for the new structure began in October of 1898 with the cornerstone being laid July 4, 1899.

Architects Charles Bell and John Kent designed the Greek Neo-Classic style building with all of the modern amenities, including electric lights, steam heat radiators, indoor plumbing, and elevators. Kent's architectural drawing of the proposed building resembled the Capitol building in South Dakota, also designed by Bell and Kent.

Utilizing the state's natural resources for building supplies, the exterior of the building was faced with sandstone from Columbus, Montana. The copper dome rises 165 feet above ground level and is topped by a bronze statue depicting a variation on Lady Liberty.

Governor Toole dedicated the new statehouse on July 4, 1902. Despite rain, the lengthy dedication ceremony included speeches by Wilbur F. Sanders, senator Paris Gibson, and Secretary of State George M. Hayes. The celebration continued the next day with a gala parade through Helena.

In 1909 the 11th legislative assembly approved the issuance of capitol bonds for the expansion of the Capitol building. Architects F.M. Andrews of New York and Link and Haire of Montana were selected to design the wing additions. Granite from Clancy, Montana was selected to face the addition rather than the softer sandstone used on the original portion of the Capitol. Construction was completed by 1912.

The Ohio firm of F. Pedretti's Sons designed the interior of the statehouse, including the stained glass windows. The scagliola columns give the appearance of solid marble but are made of plaster and hollow to accommodate electricity. Colorado's Capitol, under construction at the same time, did not include provisions for electricity as officials believed it to be a fad that would not last.

The 1935 earthquake damaged the original blue glass floor, which was replaced in the 1960s by terrazzo in the design of the state seal. The 1999–2000 restoration efforts replaced the floor with tiles in the image of the original glass.

An amber glass roof, known as the barrel vault, highlighted the grand stairway. In 1903 the State of Montana received Amédée Joullin's painting *Driving of the Golden Spike*. The painting, which depicts the completion of the transcontinental line of the Northern Pacific Railway at Gold Creek in 1883, hangs in the arch at the end of the barrel vault.

During the 1999–2000 restoration of the Capitol, the grand stairway was restored to its original splendor, complete with the removal of a false ceiling that replaced the barrel vault in 1965.

The 90-panel window was replaced in addition to the replacement of *The Driving of the Golden Spike* painting. All artwork was professionally cleaned and repaired during the restoration process.

Governor Toole requested that the Pedretti's depict the history of the state in the artwork. As a result, the four canvases at the rim of the dome are of Native-American Chief Charlo, a cowboy, miner Henry Edgar, and trapper Jim Bridger representing the four phases of early territory and state history.

The Hennessy Mercantile Company of Butte designed the furnishings and floor coverings used throughout the building. The interior boasted of the elegance and sophistication of the young state as seen in this picture taken of the governor's office and reception room in 1903.

The Capitol was also home to the Montana Historical Society library and museum. The main room of the library, pictured here in 1904, also displayed art from the museum's collection. The Montana Historical Society Museum, (opposite page, 1928), moved across the street from the Capitol into the new Veteran's Memorial Building in 1953. Bearing the responsibility of

preserving a representative selection of all historic resources important to the understanding of Montana history, the Historical Society is home to the museum, library, archives, photo archives, publications, and State Historic Preservation Office.

In 1911 cowboy artist Charles M. Russell was commissioned to paint a large mural for the then under construction House of Representatives. The 24-foot, 9-inch long and 11-foot, 5-inch wide *Lewis and Clark Meeting Indians at Ross' Hole* was Russell's largest painting and took three and half months to complete. Because of its size, Russell had to raise the roof on his log cabin studio by three logs in order for the canvas to fit. The mural depicts the September 4, 1805, meeting of the Corps of Discovery by the Salish Indians near Sula, Montana.

The 1912 Capitol addition also included the creation of a law library, pictured here in 1917; it was originally one large room with reading tables and stacks. Artist Ralph DeCamp was commissioned to paint six paintings for the library; in 1926 he completed four more murals for the room.

Renovations and use changes over the years significantly altered the appearance of the former law library. The 1999–2000 renovation did not return the space into its original function but did make the area more suitable for current needs.

The original Senate Chamber became home to the Supreme Court after the 1912 addition. The Supreme Court met in this room until the completion of the Justice Building in 1983. F. Pedretti's Sons also completed the murals for this room. Each of the seats in the galley contains a cowboy hat rack, reminding visitors of the state's western heritage.

In 1905 a statue of Thomas Francis Meagher was unveiled and dedicated on the lawn in front of the Capitol. Meagher was appointed secretary of Montana Territory in 1865 by President

Andrew Johnson and served as acting governor of the Territory under Sidney Edgerton and
Green Clay Smith.

Pictured here is the Montana State Capitol after the completion of the 1912 addition of the east and west wings. The origin of the bronze statue that adorns the copper dome is unknown. During construction of the original section of the statehouse, the statue arrived by train with no identification as to artist or sender but only the intent that it be used on the new Capitol building.

The Montana State Capitol as it appears today.

Five

THE GAY NINETIES AND BEYOND

*T*he Crash of 1893 hit Helena with force. Banks declared bankruptcy; businesses closed; people deserted the community almost as rapidly as they had appeared. By 1900 the economic center of the state had moved to Butte, and luring tourists to Helena had become virtually impossible. The Broadwater, unable to withstand such poor economic conditions, closed its doors in 1894. Never again would the hotel operate as the luxury resort for which it had been designed. Still, the natatorium remained open to local residents as a swimming area in the summer and an ice-skating rink in the winter.

Charles Broadwater's nephew, Thomas A. Marlow, assumed control of the Broadwater, along with the Colonel's various other business interests, in 1892. Marlow attempted to run the resort in the manner his uncle had designed. But despite his efforts, the hotel closed at the end of the 1894 season. The resort remained closed until 1906 due to a shrinking state population, a lack of interest, and the harsh economic realities of the 1893 crash.

Marlow sold the property to Butte businessman James J. Breen in 1906. Breen owned two other successful hotels in Washington state, both of which he had purchased as unprofitable operations. Despite uncertainty in Breen's funding sources, Helena residents held renewed expectations for the Broadwater under Breen's ownership.

Breen planned to reopen the Broadwater as a year-round resort; however, the structure had been unattended for 12 years and required massive repairs. Extensive repairs and renovations were planned, with Breen pledging to spend whatever money necessary to restore the resort to its original splendor. New pipes replaced the aging wooden pipes that carried water from the springs, and more private baths and two small plunges were added to the hotel, along with two new ballrooms. Once again, the hotel's success depended upon the railroads and their delivery of tourists to Helena.

The Broadwater reopened on January 4, 1907, in time for the beginning of the legislative session, but under a black cloud. Breen's business connections with "Copper King" F. Augustus Heinze intertwined with the hotel. It is unclear who actually owned the property, Breen or Heinze, but financial problems quickly arose. Soon after Breen purchased the Broadwater, Heinze lost all of his assets in the Crash of 1907 and subsequently in a $1 million lawsuit involving a misappropriation-of-funds accusation. His fortune crumbled and with the loss of his financial base, Heinze could neither help Breen nor save the Broadwater. Once again promises fell short, and the Broadwater Hotel, unable to meet the expectations of its city, closed its doors to the public. The aging hotel sat idle for the next nine years.

Hugh Daly, proprietor of Gregson Hot Springs (present day Fairmont Hot Springs), purchased the hotel from Breen in 1916. However, a lack of financial success and a more lucrative business offer caused Daly to return the property to Breen.

After the Breen-Heinze fiasco, a group of Helena residents established the Broadwater Hotel Company in 1920. Charles B. Power, an influential businessman, organized the company in an attempt to save the deteriorating hotel. To purchase the property, the company raised $100,000 by public subscription. Under the direction of the Broadwater Hotel Company, structural and managerial changes occurred. The BHC hired DeWitt Hutchings as manager of the hotel and its 85 employees. Hutchings had been the assistant manager of the California Missions Inn in Riverside, California.

Since attracting tourists via the railroad proved futile, the BHC added 45 cottages to the grounds to lure motor tourists. Water was piped into the cottages from the springs, and as in the hotel, electricity lit each cottage.

Despite all of the improvements and advertising, the auto-camp venture failed. Inadequate roads, along with extended travel time and a dependence on seasonal travelers, led to the failure of the Broadwater Hotel Company. Sometime in 1920, Power assumed sole ownership of the hotel. By this time, deterioration of the structures had begun. Employees of Hutchings had removed most of the elegant furnishings, and much-needed repairs and basic maintenance had been neglected for years.

The Broadwater Hotel had always been a first-class hotel, and Power closed it in 1920 rather than compromise that value. He sealed off the entire hotel except for the dining hall, and ran a restaurant out of the facility for 17 years.

The final attempt to save the deteriorating structure, and considered the last great hope, again proved futile. In the early 1940s city mayor Jack Haytin and Col. Robert T. Frederick, commander of the First Special Service Force at Fort Harrison, negotiated a $100,000 appropriation through the War Department for renovation of the hotel, the grounds, and the natatorium.

The complex, conveniently located close to Fort Harrison, would serve as a place of rest and recuperation for soldiers returning from war. The deal stipulated that after WW II the current owner would sell the Broadwater to the City of Helena for the token price of $15,000, at which time the city would assume ownership of the hotel and property. At the last minute, the Helena Chamber of Commerce vetoed the idea. It is speculated that the Chamber instead desired to use the money to build a memorial to the First Special Service Force in what is now Memorial Park.

In 1945 a miner and local resident, Norman Rogers, purchased the hotel and natatorium for $25,000. Rogers intended to renovate and update the property. If he had razed the hotel along with the natatorium in 1946, it probably would have gone completely unnoticed. A partial new roof was added to the hotel shortly after Rogers purchased it, but other than that improvement, the Broadwater sat abandoned and untouched until 1972.

In 1972 Rogers announced that the hotel would be sold at auction, piece by piece. He reasoned that trespassing had become a constant problem and that trespassers did not receive sufficient punishment. Manderville Auction Company presided over the auction on September 21 and 22, 1974. The hotel was dismantled, and the structure was razed in 1976.

Community opinion in the mid-1970s chastised Rogers for his failure to save the old hotel, and they blamed him for the structure's deterioration and its eventual demise. In truth, the hotel and surrounding property already sat in ruins when Rogers purchased it in 1945. Without a major financial commitment, nothing he, or anyone else, could have done would have saved the old hotel.

Thomas Marlow, a prominent banker in Helena for nearly 50 years, was the nephew of entrepreneur Colonel Broadwater. Marlow came to Montana in 1881 to work for his uncle at Fort McGinniss. He moved to Helena in 1890 to help reorganize his uncle's failing bank, of which he eventually became president. When the Montana National merged with Hauser's First National, Marlow was appointed president of the new First National Bank and Trust Company. In addition, Marlow played a key role in the organizing and managing of the Helena branch of the Federal Reserve Bank of Minneapolis that opened in 1921. He developed the War Finance Corporation and the Montana Livestock Finance Corporation, programs that were instrumental in helping many Montana ranchers during the Depression years. Marlow sat on the board of directors for the Great Northern Railway Company, the Montana Flour Mills of Great Falls, numerous financial institutions throughout the West, and oversaw operation of Broadwater's business affairs after his death. He invested in the construction of the Marlow Theater, the Placer Hotel, and Canyon Ferry Dam. Thomas Marlow died in 1938.

Despite the dismal success of the Broadwater Hotel and Natatorium, Helena continued to construct monuments to her progress. The Kessler Brewing Company, operated by German immigrant Nicholas Kessler, became one of the region's leading breweries. In conjunction with the brewery, Kessler owned a brickyard on the city's west side (currently the nationally known Bray Foundation Center for Ceramic Arts). The family's large brick mansion stood as a symbol of Helena's era of prosperity until its destruction by fire in the summer of 2001. The Broadwater Hotel complex can be seen in the distance.

Proud of their city's growing population and status, Helenan's often celebrated the Queen City's progress with parades. In 1890 the Robinson Circus entertained and delighted onlookers with their exhibits of rare and exotic animals as they paraded down Last Chance Gulch.

Helena's west side became the focus of development in the 1880s with the construction of the Broadwater Hotel and Natatorium, the success of the Kessler Brewing Company and Brickyard, and the early operation of State Nursery. Served by electric streetcar, the western outskirts of town became a favored destination for Helena residents. Added to this in 1895 was the opening of the magical Central Park. The magnificent grounds contained a merry-go-round, a large outdoor dance pavilion, two restaurants, two saloons, a lake for boating in the summer and ice harvesting in the winter, bowling alleys, a league-size baseball field with grandstands, picnic areas, and a zoo filled with all kinds of animals and birds. It was built by brothers Joseph and Frank Mares, longtime owners of the Central Meat Market, later renamed the Helena Meat Company. Needing acreage to handle cattle for their growing meat company, the Mares brothers purchased property west of town. Northern Pacific tracks cut through the property, where the brothers located their stable, pasture, slaughterhouse, and feedlot. On the south side of the tracks they decided to build a park reflective of Helena's growing sophistication and population. The park's grounds were used as a training facility for soldiers en route to the Spanish American War in 1898. The Green Meadow Country Club has since replaced Central Park.

Patterned after the Cathedral of Cologne, Germany and a near replica of the Votive Church of Vienna, the Cathedral of Saint Helena stands as a monument to God and tribute to the Diocese of Helena. Twin spires rise 230 feet above the ground and are topped with gold-leafed crosses 12 feet high and 6 feet across. The north tower contains 15 hand-cast bells, dedicated to the 15 mysteries of the Rosary. The interior of the cathedral features 11,693 square feet of stained glass; 59 of the windows depict Old and New Testament events and the collection represents one of the finest in the world. Twenty-nine statues depicting saints and important figures in world history grace the cathedral's limestone exterior. The cathedral dominates the local landscape watching over the Queen City of the Rockies.

The vision of Bishop John Patrick Carroll, construction of the cathedral began in 1908 and by July of 1913 the exterior of the building had been completed. Mass was celebrated in the facility for the first time on Christmas Day, 1914. The Cathedral of Saint Helena was officially consecrated on June 3, 1924, after the installation of the stained glass windows had been completed. In addition to the cathedral, Bishop Carroll also orchestrated the funding and construction of an all boys' high school in Helena. Mount Saint Charles High School eventually evolved into Carroll College, a diocesan college dedicated to the education of young men in the classics and the teachings of the Church. Today, Carroll College is a nationally ranked liberal arts college serving a student body of over 1,500.

In July of 1918 a sixth fire in downtown Helena destroyed several buildings near the Power Block on Sixth Avenue and North Main Street. The Broadwater business block was one of the many businesses destroyed by the lightning-induced fire.

Due to the repeated destruction of Helena's downtown by fire, a fire tower was erected on Tower Hill to guard the city from future destruction. The third "Guardian of the Gulch," pictured here in 1928, has been restored, renovated, and remodeled many times but still watches over the city.

Training began at Fort Harrison on July 20, 1942, for the legendary World War II First Special Service Force. The international unit was comprised of hand-picked volunteers from the U.S. and Canada. Dubbed the "Devil's Brigade," the mountain trained paratroopers specialized in sabotage, demolition, mountain climbing, and river fording. The small but fierce force suffered more than 2,300 casualties, including more than 400 killed and missing. After the war many members of the Devil's Brigade returned to make Montana their home, many settling in Helena. On April 6, 1943, members of the first section of the First Special Service Force marched through the streets of downtown Helena before hundreds of supportive and grateful citizens.

Charles B. Power, the son of influential senator and businessman T.C. Power, purchased the Broadwater in 1920 and attempted to save the deteriorating structure. His efforts proved futile and in 1938 Power sold the property to an unknown buyer. It is speculated that a relative living in California purchased the hotel and natatorium. Nonetheless, no improvements or updates were made during this time and a "for sale" sign once again adorned the once well-manicured grounds.

The BROADWATER
Hotel, Camp and Natatorium
Helena, Montana

Yellowstone and Glacier

National Parks

are

YOURS
USE THEM!

See Both Parks This Summer

and Stay for Awhile

at the

Broadwater Hotel

or

Broadwater Camp

Midway Between on the Geysers

to Glaciers Road

Helena
Montana

A DAY'S DRIVE
| TO |
GEYSERS or GLACIERS

Published by

THE BROADWATER HOTEL COMPANY

The BHC tried to attract motor tourists traveling between Glacier and Yellowstone National Parks. Advertising proclaimed that only a one-day's drive separated the hotel from either park. For tourists not wishing to drive, motor coaches stopped at the hotel daily en route between the parks. In an effort to spark tourist interest, the BHC published the "Geysers to Glaciers" brochure in 1920. Proclaiming the Broadwater the "highest class summer hotel between the Great Lakes and Del Monte, California," the BHC boasted that the "real West is about the Broadwater."

107

When Power sold the Broadwater in 1938, it was renamed the Broadwater Inn and operated as a restaurant, gambling parlor, and dance hall. Instead of targeting glamorous tourists, the Inn catered to local residents. Area advertisements proclaimed the Broadwater "Montana's most famous night club." Obnoxious, cheap neon replaced the soft tones of luxury. Slot machines lined the parlors where once fine furnishings resided. The new night club boasted such attractions as "Mal Duke and his Royal Hawaiians, performing dance music styled in Hula rhythms," not quite the caliber of entertainment that Colonel Broadwater had intended for his dream resort.

This is a memorial that was erected to the First Special Service Force in Helena. It is speculated that funds intended for the restoration of the Broadwater Hotel and Natatorium into an Old Soldiers Home were used to construct the Memorial Park swimming pool.

The aging natatorium in 1940, five years after an extended series of earthquakes rocked the Helena valley. Many Helenan's recall swimming at the natatorium long after the hotel had been closed but structural damage rendered the piscina unsafe. No longer would Colonel Broadwater's dream serve the people of the city he loved.

The 1935 quakes devastated the natatorium. After futile efforts to repair the plunge, the structure had to be demolished in 1946. Had the natatorium survived the tremors, structural weakness eventually would have rendered the plunge unsafe. Wooden fixtures, wooden pipes, and the instability of the decorative boulders spelled its demise.

A broken dream, the Broadwater hotel sat in ruins until 1972 when current owner Norman Rogers auctioned off the remaining furniture and fixtures. The Persian bathtubs of porcelain, oak chairs, velvet sofas, crystal chandeliers, European beds, marble stands, and mahogany tables were lined up along the grounds and the highway for inspection by perspective buyers. Everything from the stained-glass windows to the floorboards sold that weekend. A contractor demolished the remains in 1976.

BROADWATER
RESORT HOTEL
AUCTION

— 2 BIG DAYS —

**Saturday, September 21 and
Sunday, September 22, 1974**

10:00 a.m. — Both Days

HELENA, MONTANA

2 Miles West of Helena, on Highway 12

Owner: Norman Rogers

Sale Managed by

Mandeville Auction Service

1121 Mandeville Lane — Bozeman, Montana

John Mandeville, Auctioneer — (406) 587-7832

NOT RESPONSIBLE FOR LOSSES OR ACCIDENTS

This is a flyer from the 1974 Auction.

In 1941 a crackdown on gambling across the state and America's encroaching involvement in World War II prompted the final closure of the Broadwater. The hotel would never again open its doors and sat on the edge of town as a reminder of a by-gone era of elegance and wealth.

AT THE

Broadwater

SHARPE'S

ORCHESTRA

Every Evening

AND

Sunday Afternoon and Evening.

CAFE

IN

Connection With The Hotel.

Sunday 8 July 1894

This is a vintage flyer for an evening event at the Broadwater Hotel and Natatorium.

Six

THE BROADWATER TODAY

*T*he Broadwater hotel, once a symbol of grace and elegance, is now but a fading memory. Many Montanans claim ownership of furniture, fixtures, floorboards, doors, and windows from the old hotel. These "leftovers" serve as reminders, keeping the Broadwater alive in a small way for some. No single event is responsible for the hotel's final demise.

Realistically, the Broadwater could operate only on a seasonal basis due to the location of Helena. Harsh winters rendered travel difficult and the few guests who might be present during the winter season could not produce enough revenue to warrant remaining open.

Montana at the turn of the century claimed a population of only 243,329. The Broadwater depended upon tourists from within Montana for financial stability. Without a large population base from which to draw, the hotel's reliance on recreational travelers became problematic.

A lack of adequate transportation to the hotel created another problem for the resort. Originally, Colonel Broadwater envisioned transcontinental rail lines bringing Eastern tourists to his luxurious hotel. Unfortunately, railroads failed to bring the necessary guests and eventually mainline travel by-passed Helena. The horse-and-buggy mode of transport, while popular and stylish, proved impractical for long trips.

The automobile gained popularity both too early and too late for the Broadwater. An incomplete infrastructure made traveling long distances by car futile and uncomfortable. Primitive roads to Helena either delayed travel or crippled it. Furthermore, automobiles detracted from rail travel and failed to bring sufficient numbers of guests to the resort. By the time highways and roads had improved, the hotel had lost its luster.

In the 1970s, citizens of Helena protested the destruction of the tired and worn frame of the Broadwater; yet the passing of the hotel's grandeur over the years had gone unnoticed. The hotel sat in progressive decline at the edge of the city for decades, and few residents stopped to take note, or, if they did, they assumed that the Broadwater would last forever.

Colonel Broadwater's dream could not withstand the challenges and changes of the 20th century, nor could the hotel alter its image to meet the intentions of new owners. The Broadwater glistened as a health spa for the elite but paled in its other roles. Rather than cheapen the Colonel's intentions, the Broadwater slowly and quietly faded into the past.

This is a vintage postcard of the Broadwater Hotel and Natatorium shortly after the completion of the landscaping.

TO THE BROADWATER

"Some prescient angel softly told me
As tearless sorrow held me fast,
'A day of resurrection surely—
Its pristine glory is not past.'

With hurtful moth and baneful spider
Alone I trod thy silent hall
Where Time—Death's great derider
Was spreading wide his dusty pall.

I sadly watched thy fleeting glory,
As, Phantom-like, it fades away;
While Time and Spider spun the story;
Broadwater's seen its palmiest day.

"Full well the sturdy master builded
In wilds, Egytian-like of old,
His homely phrases were not gilded,
His plighted word was good as gold.

"Again thy fountains softly saying,
As weird the phantoms gaily flit,
'God bless our second time for playing
When Fashion's hand our lamps relit.'

"The guests regather round rejoicing;
Joy reigns supreme with laughter loud;
And all give praise, their spirits voicing
Glory to him of whom we're proud.

"From pain, disease or blighting sorrow
Stranger seekest thou relief?
Forgot thy cares be, and to-morrow
Health, Wealth and merriment achieve."

—THOMAS MURRAY SPENCER
Butte, Mont.

This is a vintage postcard of the natatorium featuring a poem to the Broadwater by Thomas Murray Spencer of Butte, Montana.

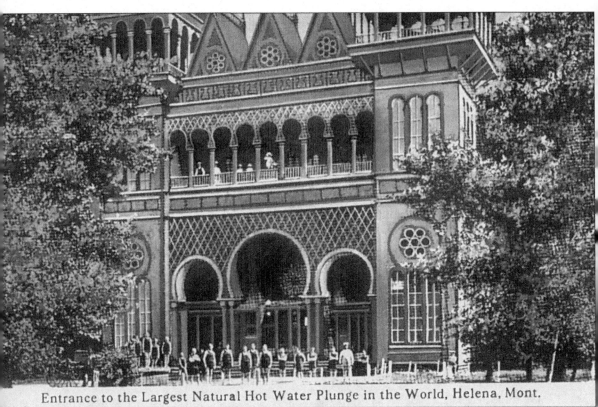

Entrance to the Largest Natural Hot Water Plunge in the World, Helena, Mont.

This vintage postcard features swimmers in front of the Natatorium. Patrons could rent bathing suites for the day. When not enjoying the waters of the plunge, guests took enjoyment from the candy store located inside the natatorium.

Pictured here is an artist's rendition of the natatorium's interior for a postcard.

The large pool at the natatorium featured a spray fountain in addition to the decorative granite bolder waterfall.

Historian Patricia Dean observed of the Broadwater's passing, "The Broadwater did not deserve such a fate, its past magnificence unappreciated, its end unobserved."

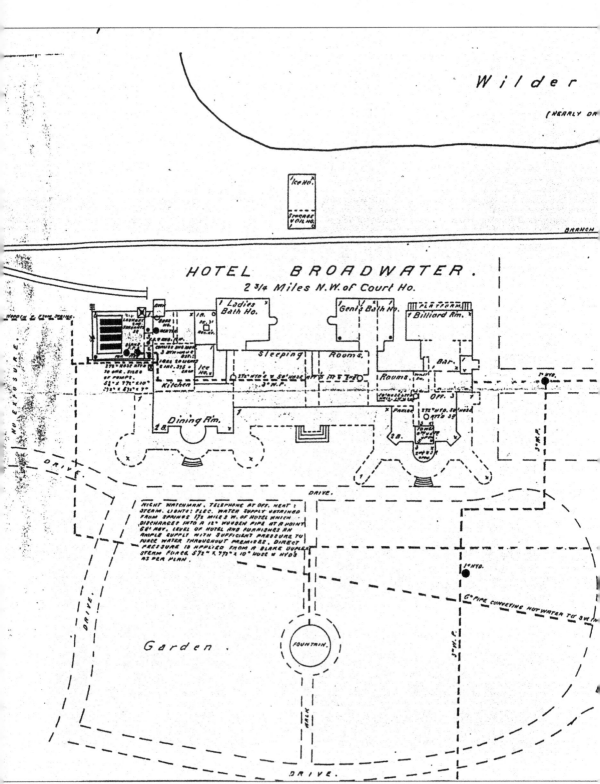

This is an 1892 Sanborn-Ferris insurance map of the Broadwater property.

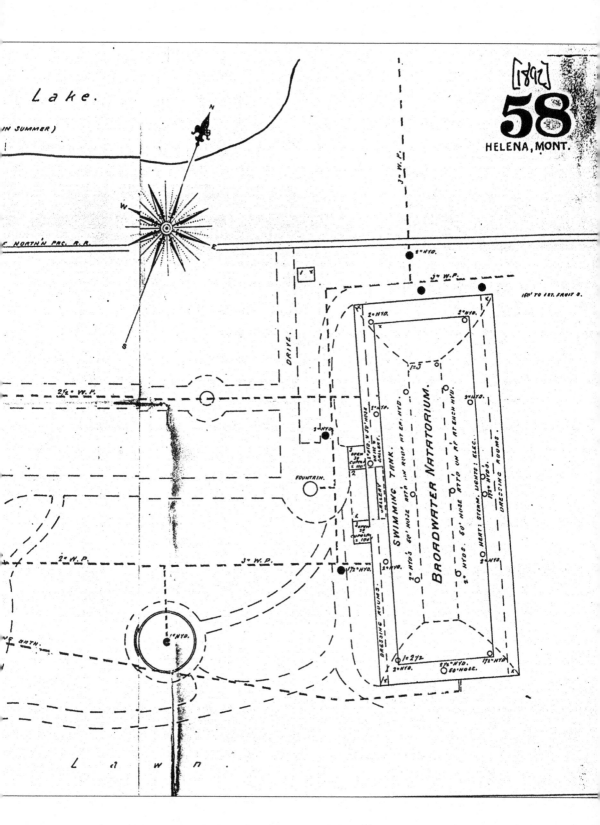

Lake.

(IN SUMMER)

N

W   E

S

F. NORTH'N PAC. R.R.

[1892]
58
HELENA, MONT.

160' TO 1ST. FRUIT S.

2½" W.P.

2" W.P.

3" W.P.

E. NORTH.

1" HYD.

FOUNTAIN.

DRIVE.

L a w n .

BROADWATER NATATORIUM.

SWIMMING TANK.

DRESSING ROOMS.

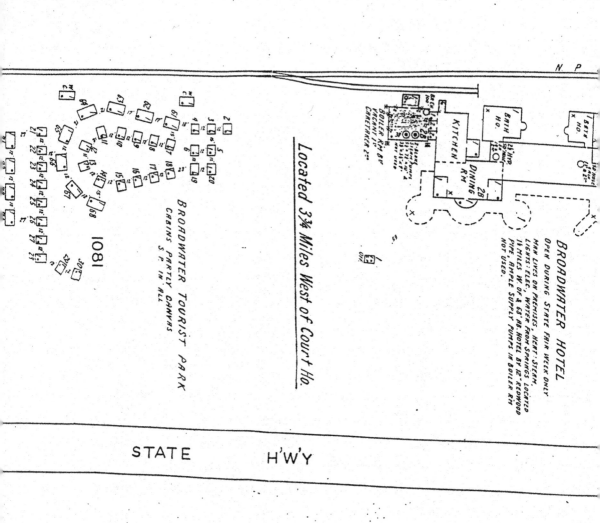

This is another Sanborn-Ferris insurance map of the Broadwater property featuring the

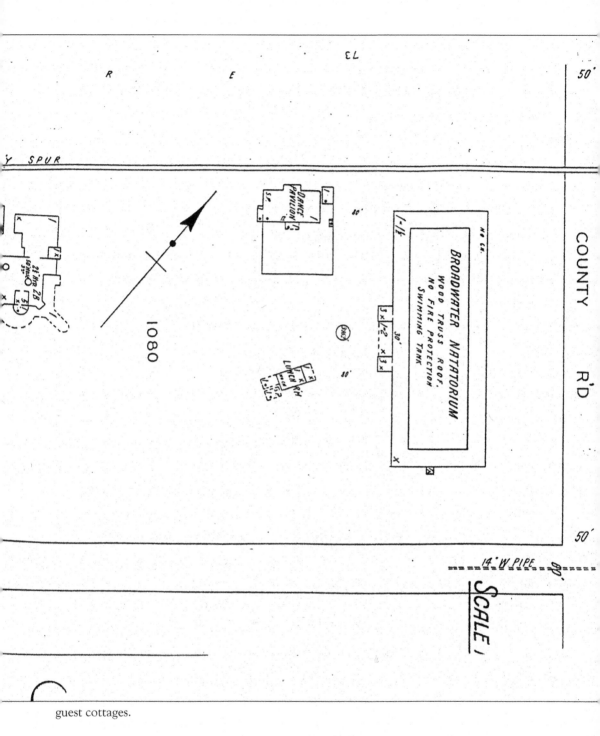

guest cottages.

PARTIAL LIST OF BROADWATER HOTEL OWNERS
FROM 1889-2001

1889: Colonel Charles A. Broadwater

1892: Thomas A. Marlow

1907: Helena Hot Springs Company, Proprs.
Henry A. Meyer, Manager

James J. Breen purchases Hotel in September

1916: Hugh Daly
George Gordon, Manager (1912-1917)

1918: James Breen
Harry Hillman, Manager

1920: James Breen
Aaron J. Little, Manager

Broadwater Hotel Company
C.B. Power member and contributor to Company
DeWitt Hutchings, Manager

Charles B. Power assumes sole control of Hotel in late
1920

1938: Power sells Hotel to unknown source (possibly a relative)

1941: Ownership unknown, possibly to same person as in 1938.

1945: Norman Rogers purchase

1995: Norman Rogers Estate

1997: Former Governor Tim & Mrs. Betty Babcock

2001: Former Governor Tim & Mrs. Betty Babcock

Here is a partial list of owners from 1889–2001.

Bibliography

The Anaconda Standard. 25 May 1892.

Baucus, Jean, and Vivian Paladin. *Helena: An Illustrated History.* Helena, Montana: Bar Wineglass Company, 1983.

Bayne, Nedra. "The Broadwater: Relic of Elegance." *Montana The Magazine of Western History.* Vol. 19 No. 3 (Summer 1969): 58–66.

Beckworth, cc, comp. *Ide's Helena City Directory for 1889.* Helena, Montana. A.W. Ide, 1889.

Bik, Patricia. Montana State Historic Preservation Office. Helena, Montana. Interview by author. 25 October 1994.

Brier, Warren J. "Helena Landmark Slumbers Today, Natatorium Gone." Montana Historical Society vertical file. Montana Historical Society Library. Helena, Montana.

Broadwater Hotel Company. "The Broadwater Hotel: Geysers to Glaciers." Helena, Montana. 1920. (Butte) *Montana Standard.* "Former Hotelman Hugh Daly Dies." 28 August 1956.

Dean, Patricia. Museum Collections Manager, Minnesota Historical Society. Interview by author, 1 November 1994.

Dean, Patricia. "True Carlsbad of America: The Broadwater Hotel and Natatorium of Helena, Montana." In *Victorian Resorts and Hotels: Essays from a Victorian Society Autumn Symposium,* ed. Richard Guy Wilson, 79–85. n.p.: The Victorian Society in America, 1982.

Department of Agriculture and Montana Publicity Commission. *Resources of Montana: The Land of Opportunity.* Washington, D.C.: GPO, 1920.

Ellingsen, John D. "The Grand Closing of the Broadwater Hotel." In *Reflections of the Past: feature articles from the Newsletter of the Montana Ghost Town Preservation Society, 1970–1983.* 15–16. Montana Historical Society vertical file. Montana Historical Society Library. Helena, Montana.

Federal Writers Project, 1938–1941. "Charles A. Broadwater Biography, 1941." *Manuscript Collection 77,* Box 33, Folder 8. Montana Historical Society Archives. Helena, Montana.

Fletcher, Bob. "Montana Melody: Last Chance Gulch." *Montana The Magazine of Western History.* Vol. 3 No. 4 (Autumn 1953): 54–55.

Great Northern Bulletin. Helena, Montana. Summer 1892. "Broadwater Hotel and Natatorium." Montana Historical Society vertical file, Montana Historical Society Library. Helena, Montana.

Gunn, Elizabeth and Elizabeth Greenfield. "The Goose that Sang: Memoirs of Violinist Fred Kuphal." *Montana The Magazine of Western History.* Vol. 27 No. 1 (Winter 1967): 20–24.

Helena Hot Springs Company. "Health for You and Pleasure Too." 1907.

Helena Daily Herald. 26 July 1888–30 May 1893.

Helena Daily Independent. 1 July 1888–23 October 1888.

Helena Daily Journal. 26 August 1890–13 January 1891.

Helena Illustrated: 1890. Helena, Montana: Frank L. Thresher for the Helena Board of Trade, 1890.

Helena Independent. "Broadwater Hotel and Natatorium." n.d. Montana Historical Society vertical file. Montana Historical Society Library. Helena, Montana.

Helena Independent. "Broadwater Sold to Breen." 15 September 1906. Montana Historical Society vertical file. Montana Historical Society Library. Helena, Montana.

Helena Daily Record. "James Breen New Owner of Broadwater Hotel." 15 September 1906. Montana Historical Society vertical file. Montana Historical Society Library. Helena, Montana.

Helena Weekly Independent. 26 July 1888–2 August 1888.

Hidy, W. Ralph, Muriel E. Hidy, and Roy B. Scott with Don L. Hofsommer. *The Great Northern Railway: A History.* Boston: Harvard Business School, 1988.

Independent Record. "The End of a Headache." 20 September 1974: 5. Montana Historical Society vertical file. Montana Historical Society Library. Helena, Montana.

Independent Record. "Want to Buy a Great Hotel?" 29 August 1974. Montana Historical Society vertical file. Montana Historical Society Library. Helena, Montana.

Independent Record. "Colonel Broadwater's Dream Sold to Highest Bidder." 22 September 1974. Montana Historical Society vertical file. Montana Historical Society Library. Helena, Montana.

Independent Record. "'Bad Boys' of the 'Good War.'" 10 August 1986. Montana Historical Society vertical file. Montana Historical Society Library. Helena, Montana.

Independent Record. "Blazes of Yore." 27 August 2000. Montana Historical Society vertical file. Montana Historical Society Library. Helena, Montana.

Independent Record. "About the Bells." 24 December 1995. Montana Historical Society vertical file. Montana Historical Society Library. Helena, Montana.

Independent Record. "Central Park: Magical place for family entertainment." 16 November 1995.

Lang, William L. "Charles A. Broadwater and the Main Chance in Montana." *Montana The Magazine of Western History.* Vol. 39 No. 3 (Summer 1989): 30–36.

Lang, William L. "Corporate Point Men and the creation of the Montana Central Railroad, 1862–67." *Great Plains Quarterly.* Vol. 10 No. 3 (Summer 1990): 152–164.

Leaphart, Susan, ed. "Frieda and Belle Fligelman: A Frontier City Girlhood in the 1890s." *Montana The Magazine of Western History.* Vol. 3 No. 3 (Summer 1982): 85–87.

Leeson, M.A. *History of Montana, 1739–1885.* Chicago: Warner, Beers and Company. 1885. "Wassweiler Hot Springs." Montana State Historic Preservation Office, Helena, Montana.

Malone, Michael P., Richard B. Roeder, and William L. Lang. *Montana: A History of Two Centuries.* Revised ed. Seattle: University of Washington Press, 1991.

McMillan, Marilyn. "'An Eldorado of Ease and Elegance': Taking the Waters at White Sulphur Springs, 1866–1904." *Montana The Magazine of Western History.* Vol. 35 No. 2 (Spring 1985): 44–45.

McNelis, Sarah. *Copper King at War.* 2nd ed. Missoula: University of Montana Press, 1968.

Miller, Robert E. "'Colonel' Broadwater's Far Flung Enterprises." *Montana Magazine.* Vol. 11 No. 5 (May–June 1981): 18–23.

Montana Historical Architectural Inventory. "Broadwater Hotel and Natatorium." State Historic Preservation Office vertical file. State Historic Preservation Office. Helena, Montana.

Montana Post: Official Newsletter of the Montana Historical Society. "Broadwater Hotel and Natatorium Helena's Pride 76 Years Ago." Vol. 3 No. 6 (June 1965). Montana Historical Society vertical file. Montana Historical Society Library. Helena, Montana.

Northern Pacific Railroad. *The Northern Pacific Railroad Brochure.* 1891.

The Northwest Illustrated Monthly Magazine. St. Paul, Minnesota. Vol. 8, No. 6 (June 1890), 21.

Power, Tom. Phone interview by author. Helena, Montana. 30 March 1995.

Progressive Men of Montana. Chicago: A.W. Bowen and Company Engravers, 1902.

Robertson, Donald B. *The Encyclopedia of Western Railroad History: the Mountain States—Colorado, Idaho, Montana, Wyoming.* Dallas: Taylor Publishing Company, 1991.

Sanders, James U. *Society of Montana Pioneers.* Constitution, Members, and Officers with Portraits and Maps. Helena, Montana: Society of Montana Pioneers, 1899.

Schroeder, John W. *Historic Helena: An Early day Photographic History of Montana's Scenic Capital City 1864–1964.* Helena, Montana: Thurber Printing Co., 1984.

(Sidney) *Richland County Leader.* "Broadwater was a Name to Conjure with in Early Days of the Treasure State." 29 April 1924. Montana Historical Society vertical file. Montana Historical Society Library. Helena, Montana.

Skidmore, Bill. *Treasure State Treasury: Montana Banks, Bankers, and Banking 1864–1984.* For the Montana Bankers Association. Helena, Montana: Thurber Printing Co., 1984.

Standish, John K. "The Adventurous Career of Charles Broadwater, who did much to win Montana from Wilderness, was head of famous Diamond R. Fought Indians and Highwaymen." *The Fergus County Argus.* 10 November 1919. Montana Historical Society vertical file. Montana Historical Society Library. Helena, Montana.

United States Department of the Interior, National Park Service, *National Register of Historic Places* Nomination Form. "Wassweiler Hot Springs," Montana State Historic Preservation Office, Helena, Montana.

Walter, Dave. *Today Then.* Helena, Montana: American & World Geographic Publishing, 1992.

White, Thomas W. "The War of the Railroad Kings: Great Northern-Northern Pacific Rivalry in Montana, 1881–1896." *Montana and the West: Essays in Honor of K. Ross Toole.* Edited by Rex C. Meyers and Harry W. Fritz. Boulder, Colorado: Pruett Publishing Company, 1984.

Williams, Pat. "The Devil's Brigade: Remembering the Heros." *A Message for Western Montana.* October 1989.

CPSIA information can be obtained
at www.ICGtesting.com
Printed in the USA
LVOW05*1012220916

505761LV00014B/69/P